ISBN= 8387929336

ABOUT THE AUTHOR

I am Adam Mogul, some say "Adam of Cambridgeshire".

I spent most of my life in Dubai, right from childhood until my mid 20s when I moved country to country, from town to town looking for a home but somehow never managing to find a place where I felt that I belonged. Along the way I met some interesting people and some who were not so nice...

Life happened, with its ups and downs, with fascinating moments full of love and joy, and heartbreaking moments of sadness and loneliness...

Strangely, I never knew how to express my feelings or thoughts and then I worked

W0009880

really hard at expressing myself and now I talk non-stop, mostly nonsense...

People who know me well say that I am full of life, I say I am full of emotions.

I spent most of my days working and my nights either in silence or socialising...

This is my 7th year in England, United Kingdom and I recently moved to Cromer, a beautiful seaside town and decided to start writing my thoughts...

I would say majority of this book was written sitting on the sand at the beach with sound of waves in the sea as my background orchestra... some tears were shed, some smiles took over too...

I always say that us humans
are emotional beings, we are full
of emotions, so much so that we
were even conceived because of
emotions and in this book I tried
expressing myself the best
I could and for you to know that
you are not alone, you are not
alone anymore in the thoughts
that you live in...

Feel free to add me on social
media, all of my links will be
mentioned on the last page...

I hope you enjoy reading this
book with a smile and its okay to
shed a tear or two too......

A Journey Through My Silence
by Adam Mogul

My world shifted
the moment I saw you for
the first time.

I was never the same again....

A Journey Through My Silence
by Adam Mogul

O nce so full of life, now
disappointed and hollow...

A Journey Through My Silence
by Adam Mogul

E ven before we had
crossed paths, I longed for you.
A longing so great it both
haunted and excited me...

I saw in your eyes
both my beginning and
my end...

B eing held in your arms
was my heaven...
and now its gone...

A Journey Through My Silence
by Adam Mogul

I pretend your absence doesn't bother me...

But inside, I am torn apart...

From the instant we met,
I was aware not having you
around would be agony...

You will remain in my heart, an eternal dream of love...

Why not?

A question that tears my heart everyday...

A Journey Through My Silence
by Adam Mogul

In my darkest hour,
I felt alone...
until you showed up and
filled the void...

You bring back memories
of my past self, the person
I used to be before you left...

My empty, echoing
footsteps serve as a reminder
of what I once had...
YOU.
I am lost in a solemn dance
with my memories...

A Journey Through My Silence
by Adam Mogul

They foolishly say time
cannot be stopped...
But every time I kissed you
my time stopped...

It felt like heaven...

Everything's okay -
I whispered.

An empty lie within a
broken heart...

A Journey Through My Silence
by Adam Mogul

My longing for you
becomes unbearable when
night draws near.

I cannot help but think of your
precious face...

A Journey Through My Silence
by Adam Mogul

A gentle breeze susurrate the trees, sweetly stealing away their leaves, as I restlessly ponder you...

I remember,

I remember,

I remember how perfectly
you fit in my arms...

A Journey Through My Silence
by Adam Mogul

Though time passes, memories of you will remain forever in my heart.
I cannot forget the places we met, your face, your touch, your voice, the fragrance of you...

A Journey Through My Silence
by Adam Mogul

Tonight we met for the
very first time...
A timeless moment, sealed
with an everlasting kiss...

A Journey Through My Silence
by Adam Mogul

With my heart filled to the brim with love for you, there is no room left inside it for me...

I will meet you again,
tonight... like every night...

Transformed to strangers,
a heartbreaking burden...

M y love for you is limitless...
A forever reminder of moments together...

For years, I prayed to the universe to send someone who is you...
The day you walked into my life I realised I had met my match...

M y dream came true...
but I am devastated not to
have the chance to live it with
you...

A Journey Through My Silence
by Adam Mogul

L onging for you is a
darkness I cannot shake.
My heart aches with the desire
to see your face again...

A Journey Through My Silence
by Adam Mogul

With just a glance, I saw
something special in your soul,
an undeniable connection
beyond the surface...

A Journey Through My Silence
by Adam Mogul

I dreamed of lifelong romance with you, and that someday, you would make my dream come true...

A Journey Through My Silence
by Adam Mogul

I am so occupied on so
many fronts, I often get so very
tired, so disheartened, daunted
and deterred,
but with you, my darling,
by my side...
I promise I will conquer the
world.

In my arms is where
you belong...
in your arms is where
I belong...

A Journey Through My Silence
by Adam Mogul

I cherished you more than words can convey. With tireless devotion, my only wish was to wallow in the sparkling beauty of the heavens above. But they remain just out of reach...

Memories of your face
linger in my heart,
never fading no matter how
time passes.
A priceless portrait that can
never be replaced...

A Journey Through My Silence
by Adam Mogul

With each passing day
new hope is born, but without
you by my side,
this is an empty sunrise...

A Journey Through My Silence
by Adam Mogul

You are the worst pain
I have ever had in my life,
yet you are the best comfort
I will ever have in my life...

Always I will be there.
A warm embrace to soothe
your soul until the very,
last breath...

A Journey Through My Silence
by Adam Mogul

With you, my heart finds its rhythm. You are the source of all I create, a constant presence in my thoughts and dreams - my muse, an endless fountain of inspiration...

A Journey Through My Silence
by Adam Mogul

I face the world like a lion
but standing before you I melt
like snow in sunshine...

A Journey Through My Silence
by Adam Mogul

In the tenderness of our kisses, I felt a stirring of mortality, it was as if all life and death were there...

A Journey Through My Silence
by Adam Mogul

My heart longs to be filled with joy and happiness. Instead, there is a hollow ache burrowed deep within that you have left me with...

A Journey Through My Silence
by Adam Mogul

C old and empty,
my heart is frozen in the
depth of winter...
A single touch from you would
thaw it like ice on an
April morning...

A Journey Through My Silence
by Adam Mogul

You ignited the darkness
with a passionate flame,
one of an intensity that I had
never seen before...

No other fire burning in my
world could compete with
yours...

No light blazed brighter than
you...

A Journey Through My Silence
by Adam Mogul

L ying alone in the dark,
a single thought comes to my
mind...
you, in a white tank top.
you, smiling with kind eyes.
you, whispering,
"I am all yours"

A Journey Through My Silence
by Adam Mogul

Sitting in a crowded room
so very full of beautiful
people... and here I am,
head down scrolling through
your pictures...

A Journey Through My Silence
by Adam Mogul

They think I live my life for the riches and for fame... but all I want is simply to be happy and happy is to be with you...

A Journey Through My Silence
by Adam Mogul

My love for you pulses
through my veins,
constant and faithful.
You're the spark that ignites
my creativity.
I express these words with
passion, because of you...

W ith you by my side,

life is real. Everything is rich
and full and perfect when I am
living it with you...

A Journey Through My Silence
by Adam Mogul

Your smile is enough to stir a sea of emotion in me, an overwhelming surge, a deluge that cannot be contained...

A Journey Through My Silence
by Adam Mogul

I have been intoxicated by my love for you and I do not wish to sober up...

Without you, I survive. I wish I could hold you again so that I might stop surviving and start living once again...

A Journey Through My Silence
by Adam Mogul

With each step I feel the
pain of aching feet,
yet my heart aches more from
years of unrequited love...

A Journey Through My Silence
by Adam Mogul

Our eyes met and the world seemed to shift.
In that moment,
I knew my life would never be
the same again...

A Journey Through My Silence
by Adam Mogul

Love lost is a deep sorrow that lingers, a shadow of what could have been....

A Journey Through My Silence
by Adam Mogul

Even on the darkest night, I look up at the sky, hoping that somewhere you are looking up at that same sky...

A Journey Through My Silence
by Adam Mogul

You lovingly administered my death, and I accepted it without hesitation...

A Journey Through My Silence
by Adam Mogul

I cried with a smile on my
face, my lips saying,
"it's time to move on",
but the truth is that I just can't
leave you behind...

A Journey Through My Silence
by Adam Mogul

E ven the most promising
of beginnings can be snuffed
out with suddenness,
leaving nothing but memories
and a sense of what could have
been...

A Journey Through My Silence
by Adam Mogul

After experiencing love,
nothing was ever the same;
I had been irrevocably
transformed...

A Journey Through My Silence
by Adam Mogul

The sweetest promise or harshest goodbye carries it all, a duality of joy and sorrow that never fails to leave its mark...

A Journey Through My Silence
by Adam Mogul

You were the charming
embodiment of potential,
sparking a world of romance in
your gaze...

A Journey Through My Silence
by Adam Mogul

How can I open my heart to the possibility of loving someone new when every night I still pine for you?

A Journey Through My Silence
by Adam Mogul

Those eyes gazed into
mine with an infinity of love,
promising a future together
as though it was meant to be...

I am helplessly in love.
My every thought revolves
around you.
It is beyond my control...

A Journey Through My Silence
by Adam Mogul

I thought "I'll move to a new place and everything with be fine." How wrong I was.

Now I miss you even more...

A Journey Through My Silence
by Adam Mogul

I lost myself in your eyes
and that was the end of my
existence as me...

Could it be that my tenderness was simply insufficient against the harshness of the world?

A Journey Through My Silence
by Adam Mogul

All I wish for is your presence, nothing more and nothing less.
No enchanting tale can replace the warmth of your embrace...

A Journey Through My Silence
by Adam Mogul

I f only I had put walls around my heart, I would not have known the pain of this broken "I love you."

A Journey Through My Silence
by Adam Mogul

I send my voice into emptiness, hoping to receive a response from your soul.

Is no one there?

A Journey Through My Silence
by Adam Mogul

With every nightfall,
I am swallowed by the desire
for you and, as my eyes close,
you fill my dreams. I am free in
my sleep to be with the one
who has captivated me...

A Journey Through My Silence
by Adam Mogul

I look in your eyes and
drift away into a web of
emotions,
I don't want to go back to being
without you,
I just want to keep looking at
you...

A Journey Through My Silence
by Adam Mogul

My thoughts chase you
in the day...
And in the night when I get
tired and shut my eyes,
you appear like magic to hold
me in your arms...

A Journey Through My Silence
by Adam Mogul

One day as I drove past,
I saw red roses in your
window...
I can't remember hearing
myself ever cry so loud...

I still feel that pain...

A Journey Through My Silence
by Adam Mogul

If only I could turn the clock back and whisper a gentle reassurance that all will be forgiven...

A Journey Through My Silence
by Adam Mogul

M

y final moment.
Me, clinging desperately to a
doomed vessel.
The end of my voyage...

A Journey Through My Silence
by Adam Mogul

Even in the night sky,
my thoughts still drift to you.
I yearn for your presence
beneath a blanket of stars...

Why should I settle for less?

You are my treasure,
worth more than any gold...

A Journey Through My Silence
by Adam Mogul

All I had were simple words and you came into my life and added music to it. Now I sit in silence singing songs about you...

A Journey Through My Silence
by Adam Mogul

Ⅰn my embrace I held a
piece of heaven.
The moment felt eternal when
I was with you...

A Journey Through My Silence
by Adam Mogul

My heart ached for the love I felt for you.
An echo of a distant memory that lingers in my dreams...

A Journey Through My Silence
by Adam Mogul

With no one to hear them, my words lay silent in the shadows of my soul...

A Journey Through My Silence
by Adam Mogul

I took the emotions you had stirred in me.

I sat on the sand and began to write.

Writing and writing and writing.

Soon, I realised I had written you into a book of pure and beautiful memories...

A Journey Through My Silence
by Adam Mogul

As I walked through the
forest today, I heard the leaves
falling and the breeze
whispering your name.
It felt so real, words cannot
explain...

A Journey Through My Silence
by Adam Mogul

I remember every inch of you...

A Journey Through My Silence
by Adam Mogul

Yearning to speak,
yet unable to say a word...
Unspoken emotions swirling in
my heart...

A Journey Through My Silence
by Adam Mogul

My passion for you may
briefly lift me, but the way
things are tears my heart
apart...

A Journey Through My Silence
by Adam Mogul

All I wanted was "now",
I never even thought of
forever...
But you even took that "now"
from me...

A Journey Through My Silence
by Adam Mogul

My heart was craving sweet, yet you offered me a bitter poison.
I embraced the darkness and drank it willingly, a fool in love with my own demise...

A Journey Through My Silence
by Adam Mogul

I have been tumbling
head over heels with no end in
sight since I met you.
My feelings for you just keep
on deepening...

A Journey Through My Silence
by Adam Mogul

Forever can elicit the deepest joy or plunge us into despair.
A single word with infinite possibilities...

A Journey Through My Silence
by Adam Mogul

O ur hearts yearned for
what our eyes once saw, but
time and fate have forever
altered the union of those
meaningful glances...

A Journey Through My Silence
by Adam Mogul

We seek out emotions that will eventually break us apart, yet we never give up our search...

A Journey Through My Silence
by Adam Mogul

Y‍ou were a breathtaking masterpiece of possibility, your beauty radiating like the light from stars in a midnight sky...

A Journey Through My Silence
by Adam Mogul

Even though we are
apart, I feel a connection
beneath the star-filled
night sky.
A bittersweet smile creeps
across my face...

A Journey Through My Silence
by Adam Mogul

Yesterday I dreamed of a beautiful new dawn, yet today darkness has fallen and my world has gone...

A Journey Through My Silence
by Adam Mogul

Autumn's hues of orange and red stir nostalgia in me. The falling leaves whisper your name...

I had nearly given up on hope until our paths crossed and you filled my heart with love. It was a miracle...

A Journey Through My Silence
by Adam Mogul

When these strangers
break me and hurt me, I go out
looking for you like a child,
hoping that you'll hold me and
tell me that everything will be
just fine...

A Journey Through My Silence
by Adam Mogul

Nothing hurts more
deeply than the loss of
something beloved.
These wounds carve a path
to our core...

A Journey Through My Silence
by Adam Mogul

When the shadows of despair befall me, I search for a glimmer of your light to guide my way...

A Journey Through My Silence
by Adam Mogul

I longed for someone like
you all my life and after an
eternity of searching,
you arrived.
Yet I sit here waiting for you
every day and every night...

I cover myself in a blanket of thoughts of you, letting my pen translate them into words...

A Journey Through My Silence
by Adam Mogul

Desperate to express
untold feelings, yet held back
by a quiet neutrality,
my heart aches with emotion
but is muted by its sorrow...

Love is an emotion too
vast to verbalise, comprised of
four letters but overflowing
with more meaning than can
be captured within one word...

S eeking solace in emotions that will ultimately bring ruin, we pursue in vain an elusive joy...

A Journey Through My Silence
by Adam Mogul

With just a single word,
'forever' can ignite within us
the greatest joys or plunge us
into heart-breaking sadness...

Your passion burned like fire, your eyes radiating an unconditional love...

A Journey Through My Silence
by Adam Mogul

A light in the night sky,
you illuminated your own path,
an untouchable,
shining beacon of hope...

A Journey Through My Silence
by Adam Mogul

E ven before we had the
chance to cross paths,
my heart ached for your
presence...

A Journey Through My Silence
by Adam Mogul

My fragile heart was
simply too easy to shatter.
It broke into a hundred pieces.
You left me alone to put it all
back together...

A Journey Through My Silence
by Adam Mogul

G lancing back, faded
lines remain, reminders of the
time our eyes had locked in
desire...

A Journey Through My Silence
by Adam Mogul

As we moved together,
time stood still and all sadness
disappeared.
I felt only joy in that moment.
My worries evaporated in your
presence...

A Journey Through My Silence
by Adam Mogul

My heart was sealed,
but you crept into its fortress.
No matter how high I raised
the walls, your presence still
found a way inside...

A Journey Through My Silence
by Adam Mogul

I dreamed of being a part
of you, believing that deep
within you existed universes
unknown...

A Journey Through My Silence
by Adam Mogul

My heart aches,
wanting to be heard.
If my broken body could only
whisper, it would speak the
words I am too scared to say.
"I love you."

E ven in the most distant
corners of my imagination,
I can never escape this
all-consuming love for you...

A Journey Through My Silence
by Adam Mogul

My world feels empty,
as if the colours of my life have
faded, because I miss you.

I miss you so very much...

Loneliness and longing
became my constant
companions, burying me in
thoughts of you.
All I can do is be lost
within you, without you...

I choose you over
everyone else, again and again
and over again...

A Journey Through My Silence
by Adam Mogul

F alling for you was a heart-wrenching journey of sweet agony.

Like watching the sun set knowing that it will never rise again...

Each night I yearn for you even in my sleep. How can I give myself to someone new when my heart belongs to you...

A Journey Through My Silence
by Adam Mogul

I am surrounded by strangers, my eyes constantly searching for you...

My heart longed for
love without permission.
I find myself constantly
drifting toward thoughts of you
no matter how I try to veer
away...

A Journey Through My Silence
by Adam Mogul

Love has bewitched my
heart with an illness, a malady
of emotion unlike any other,
so profound it touches the very
depth of my soul...

A Journey Through My Silence
by Adam Mogul

I never possessed you yet
your absence cuts like a
sword...

From inception to conclusion, so much can happen in a moment. Life is fleeting and fragile...

Love may not always
make sense, but it never fails
to touch our hearts...

A Journey Through My Silence
by Adam Mogul

My love was fleeting,
almost unreal, but I adored you
so deeply.
Now I realise I loved you for so
very long that it feels like an
endless dream...

Life is incomplete
without you.
My days begin and end with
craving you...

A Journey Through My Silence
by Adam Mogul

My feelings will remain eternal. Nothing can extinguish the way I care for you. Not even death itself...

A Journey Through My Silence
by Adam Mogul

Though I wander through
a world without you,
my heart still yearns for you...

A Journey Through My Silence
by Adam Mogul

Your words pierced my
heart like an arrow, leaving me
motionless in anguish,
leaving me lost,
so very lost...

A Journey Through My Silence
by Adam Mogul

My heart aches.
I feel powerless without you.
A life saddled with the blues
because of how I feel for you...

A Journey Through My Silence
by Adam Mogul

Those eyes were timeless. In them I saw an eternity of love...

A Journey Through My Silence
by Adam Mogul

My heart knew it had
found its match,
the thought of you appearing
unhidden in my mind,
no matter how hard I tried to
forget...

We met and the world was reset.
Suddenly we were full of hope and optimism, revitalised by discovering one another's presence...

You were
My Happy Place...

A Journey Through My Silence
by Adam Mogul

Yesterday held such
promise, new life in sight.
Today is a nightmare,
devoid of all light...

A Journey Through My Silence
by Adam Mogul

Love and heartbreak are intertwined forces, inseparably and poetically linked.
Each brings the deepest joys and darkest sorrows to one's soul. A bittersweet union that is never fully understood or undone...

A Journey Through My Silence
by Adam Mogul

Our eyes met in passion,
leaving scars that remain
forever on my heart...

A Journey Through My Silence
by Adam Mogul

You filled my empty heart
with memories that I didn't
believe to merely look
back on...

A Journey Through My Silence
by Adam Mogul

Deceitful whispers, forever tugging at my heartstrings and reminding me of you...

A Journey Through My Silence
by Adam Mogul

There are so many
beautiful people in the world
but to me you are the most
beautiful of all...

A Journey Through My Silence
by Adam Mogul

L onging for you pierces me in silent lament, robbing my vision of all beauty...

A Journey Through My Silence
by Adam Mogul

We recklessly hunt for emotions that will inevitably eventually crush us, leaving only heartbreak and sorrow...

A Journey Through My Silence
by Adam Mogul

In the depths of my soul,
I felt an unconditional love for
you. Falling in love was
effortless and, just like that,
I slipped away into a blissful
abyss with only thoughts of us
together echoing throughout
my mind...

Y ou weren't the key to
my troubles, but you made me
think they never existed...

A Journey Through My Silence
by Adam Mogul

Falling for you was
effortless, like I was meant to
be with you forever, and ever...

E ven in my darkest
moments, I found a spark
of hope in your presence...

A Journey Through My Silence
by Adam Mogul

A heartache etched in
time,
a memory that will never fade.
The recollection of you....

A Journey Through My Silence
by Adam Mogul

As I felt the weight of my loneliness, I heard a faint whisper: "the longing is real".

We are all fragments of a greater puzzle, searching for our missing pieces...

A Journey Through My Silence
by Adam Mogul

We were two ships passing in the night, so close and yet so far apart, our lives marked by the steady rhythm of "almost".
How near we had come to forever together...

A Journey Through My Silence
by Adam Mogul

Love and heartache are
the two facets of life.
They come, hand in hand,
bringing joy as well as sorrow.
One cannot exist without the
other, even if our hearts may
wish it otherwise...

A Journey Through My Silence
by Adam Mogul

I have never said goodbye
to you, and I will never say
goodbye to you.
For as long as my heart beats,
it will keep taking your name.
As long as my eyes see,
they keep will searching for
you...

A Journey Through My Silence
by Adam Mogul

From miles away, my love
for you is capable of hearing
your laughter...

Those who appear to love nothing were once deeply devoted, but their hearts were broken beyond repair by that one person...

My heart ached endlessly, hoping to find a spark in your eyes that was meant for me...

A Journey Through My Silence
by Adam Mogul

A new beginning was beckoning and you stood before me, a symbol of love that inspired hope for the future...

A Journey Through My Silence
by Adam Mogul

Though I never truly had
you, an empty void remains,
a clear reminder of the loss
that will forever haunt me...

A Journey Through My Silence
by Adam Mogul

You gave me a reason to live again and so very quickly you gave me a reason to die again...

My heart is forever longing for you.
I deeply miss your warm embrace...

Love may shatter your world, leaving nothing but a broken heart and an uncertain future...

A Journey Through My Silence
by Adam Mogul

When the night grows long and lonely, sow tiny stars of hope in its pitch-black sky...

I see your perfection
through all of your
imperfections...

A Journey Through My Silence
by Adam Mogul

My days are empty without you. I cannot dream of anything sweeter than your loving embrace. Longing for the day when our eyes will meet again and to experience a reunion with your precious smile...

Your smile is a whispered promise of the love I've always desired. An alluring vision of perfect togetherness...

A Journey Through My Silence
by Adam Mogul

I drift from person to person like a falling leaf, hoping that one day you'll pick me up and put me safely in your book...

A Journey Through My Silence
by Adam Mogul

I often wonder how you could not see the depth of my love for you...

A Journey Through My Silence
by Adam Mogul

An unspoken secret,

a sad tale of love,

that is me...

A Journey Through My Silence
by Adam Mogul

While the world moves on, my heart remains with you. Each morning I am pulled in opposite directions, longing to experience new love yet unable to separate from the dreams of us that fill each night...

Time passes,
but pain lingers...

A Journey Through My Silence
by Adam Mogul

L ifetimes pass in a blink,
yet still we endure thousands
of deaths until our very last...

I had big dreams,
but you shattered them in just
one blow...

A Journey Through My Silence
by Adam Mogul

D espite the passage of
time, our sorrows remain...

A Journey Through My Silence
by Adam Mogul

My words are nothing
but blood from invisible
wounds...

A Journey Through My Silence
by Adam Mogul

Love transformed everything, including me. It took a broken soul and made it whole again, each moment filled with an emotion that could never be replaced...

A Journey Through My Silence
by Adam Mogul

My heart shattered,
and the heavens rained tears
when I saw you with somebody
else...

A Journey Through My Silence
by Adam Mogul

Restless night after night, yet not wanting to tell you how I feel...

A Journey Through My Silence
by Adam Mogul

I have everything but
without you my heart and
hands are empty...

A Journey Through My Silence
by Adam Mogul

Time stops every time I look into your eyes...

A Journey Through My Silence
by Adam Mogul

You were my anchor in a storm and I held you in my arms in your most breaking moments...

Tears are memories carried away from an aching soul...

A Journey Through My Silence
by Adam Mogul

As I grow older, I realise
I have died a hundred times in
one lifetime...

I dared to dream of a future where love was eternal...

Love transformed the world, myself included.
It altered me, for better and for worse, in ways I never thought possible...

A Journey Through My Silence
by Adam Mogul

A home for a lost soul,
you were my home...

A Journey Through My Silence
by Adam Mogul

I wanted to savour every moment, so that no regrets would haunt me...

A Journey Through My Silence
by Adam Mogul

I was yours, the very first moment I saw you...

A Journey Through My Silence
by Adam Mogul

You were the most
perfect dream that I never
wanted to wake up from...

A Journey Through My Silence
by Adam Mogul

Though the bleakest night may shroud me, a glimmer of you remains to comfort me, a whisper in my heart that assures me your presence exists.
Always there and never forgotten, hidden just beyond the drifting clouds...

A Journey Through My Silence
by Adam Mogul

An unrelenting sadness
lingers, never fading away...

A Journey Through My Silence
by Adam Mogul

G azing up at the night sky, my heart longs for the tenderness of your embrace...

A Journey Through My Silence
by Adam Mogul

I am sorry that I have
cursed you with a heart full of
pain and eyes full of tears,
screaming in my silence that
you will never find comfort
within any arms but mine,
the arms that you once called
your happy place...

A Journey Through My Silence
by Adam Mogul

You were beyond my imagination and wildest fantasies...

No happily ever after needed. All I desire is you. There is no happy ending without you...

A Journey Through My Silence
by Adam Mogul

I never imagined that love could be real until you showed me that time could stand still...

A Journey Through My Silence
by Adam Mogul

M y love for you will
never fade, an eternal feeling
that can never be replaced...

A Journey Through My Silence
by Adam Mogul

In search of an everlasting bond, I yearn for a lifetime with you...

A Journey Through My Silence
by Adam Mogul

Forever is the timeless touch of love in a single moment...

A Journey Through My Silence
by Adam Mogul

I knew that you did not belong to me yet the pain of losing you lingers in my heart...

A Journey Through My Silence
by Adam Mogul

Was I too gentle or was the world just too unyielding?

Y ou are the most
beautiful witch I will ever
meet. Period!

A Journey Through My Silence
by Adam Mogul

They all say, "he enters the room and makes everyone laugh", but no one ever thinks that they have never seen him laugh...

Even though you are not with me, I still smile at the thought that you exist...

A Journey Through My Silence
by Adam Mogul

Y ou once said,

"you know I will always come

back to you."

So, I waited...

I wait...

And I will be waiting...

A Journey Through My Silence
by Adam Mogul

Now who will love you so very much that he will write a whole, damn book about you?

A Journey Through My Silence
by Adam Mogul

I left your town thinking
it'll all stop hurting. I left those
streets behind thinking
I'll forget you.
And look at me, here, miles
away, writing your name in the
sand next to mine...

Y ou thought that I was an addict. Shame you never realised I was only addicted to you...

A Journey Through My Silence
by Adam Mogul

Every time you broke
down in tears I came running.
I bet you'll never forget that...

A Journey Through My Silence
by Adam Mogul

I have left some pieces of
my broken heart with you.
Keep them safe in your
treasure chest. Don't bury
them yet. I'm still alive,
my heart still beats.
Every time you open that
chest, you'll hear my heart
calling your name,
again, again and over again...

A Journey Through My Silence
by Adam Mogul

Ⅰf I come across love
again,
I'll look it in the eye,
I'll smile at it,
I'll take a deep breath and
I'll walk on by...

DEDICATION

S hhhh...

I be hush hush... :)

You can find me on the following social media platforms:

Facebook:
facebook.com/IamAdamMogul

@IamAdamMogul

Instagram:
@AdamMogul

TikTok:
@AdamMogul

Let's connect...